# Coretta King

### A Woman of Peace

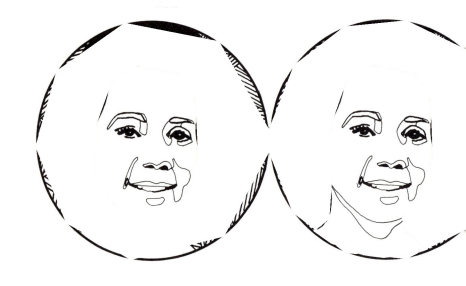

# Coretta King
## A Woman of Peace

by Paula Taylor
illustrated by Harold Henriksen

Creative Education
Mankato, Minnesota 56001

Published by Creative Education, 123 South Broad Street,
P. O. Box 227, Mankato, Minnesota 56001
Copyright © 1974 by Creative Education. No part of this book may be reproduced
in any form without written permission from the publisher. International copyrights
reserved in all countries. Printed in the United States.
Distributed by Childrens Press. 1224 West Van Buren Street, Chicago, Illinois 60607
Library of Congress Numbers: 74-17360     ISBN: 0-87191-410-7

Library of Congress Cataloging in Publication Data
Taylor, Paula.     Coretta Scott King.
SUMMARY: A brief biography of the wife of the slain civil
rights leader, Martin Luther King, Jr.
1. King, Coretta Scott, 1927-     —Juvenile literature.
[1. King, Coretta Scott, 1927-     2. Negroes—Civil rights.
3. Negroes—Biography]     I. Henriksen, Harold, illus.     II. Title.
E185.97.K47T39     323.4'092'4 [B] [92] 74-17360
ISBN 0-87191-410-7

## Introduction

When Coretta Scott King was growing up in Alabama, it was difficult for black children to finish grade school. Yet she not only graduated from college, but also took a degree in music from the famous New England Conservatory.

When she met Martin Luther King, she decided that helping other black people gain their freedom was more important than her own success. She gave up a promising concert career to marry him. Since then, she had devoted her talents to the civil rights movement, hoping that her children would not have to suffer the injustices she did.

For this she was willing to risk great danger, even death. In the end she paid a supreme sacrifice. Her husband died, defending his dream of justice for all. Yet his dream still lives. Coretta has bravely carried on the work he began. Her courage has gained her the admiration of people around the world.

Coretta King A Woman
of Peace

Coretta slowly hung up the phone. One look at her face told her sister Edythe something was wrong.

"What is it, Corrie?" she asked.

"They've burned our house down," Coretta said slowly. "Our beautiful furniture — it's all gone."

The two sisters looked at each other in dismay. For 9 years the family had lived in a house with just 2 small rooms — a kitchen and a bedroom. The floors were bare pine, and the paper was peeling off the walls. Water had to be carried in from the well in the back yard.

Finally their father had saved enough to rent a 6-room house. To Edythe and Coretta it seemed like a palace. They had a bedroom all their own. There was a living room with fine new furniture. Now it was all gone.

"Think how bad Daddy must feel," said Edythe.

Coretta nodded, her eyes filling with tears. "Poor Daddy, he's worked so hard."

The whole Scott family had worked hard. Edythe, Coretta, and their younger brother Obie all got up at dawn to feed the chickens and hogs, and milk the cows before they went to school. In the summer they and their mother tended their large vegetable garden. The children worked for neighbors, chopping and picking cotton to help pay their school expenses.

But their father had worked hardest of all. Besides running the farm, he worked long hours at a lumber mill. He had also opened a small barber shop in their home. When, at last, he'd saved enough money to buy a truck, he started hauling lumber for the mill operator at night and on weekends.

Then the trouble had started. Obie Scott was the only black man in Perry County, Alabama, who owned a truck. White truck owners started grumbling about "that uppity nigger who don't know his place." They were afraid Obie Scott would take business away from them.

White men began stopping Mr. Scott on lonely roads. Sometimes they waved guns in his face and threatened to kill him. He never ran away. He didn't stop hauling lumber, either. But when he left home to work in the woods, Coretta often heard him warn her mother, "I may not get back."

Coretta's eyes shone with pride, thinking how brave her father was. Then she remembered the fire. She was sure the white men who had threatened her father had set it, but she knew it would do no good for him to ask the sheriff to investigate. No one cared what happened to black people.

"Why do white people treat us this way?" Coretta asked herself angrily. She could find no answer. She tried to remember the first time she realized that there were places she couldn't go and things she couldn't do because of the color of her skin.

She remembered going to the movies. She had to sit in the hot, crowded balcony, while white children sat in comfortable seats on the main floor.

She remembered going to the drugstore for an ice cream cone. She and the other black children had to enter the store by the side door. White children used the front door. She had to wait until all the white people were served before the man behind the counter turned to her. Then, no matter what flavor she asked for, the man always gave her the kind he had too much of.

"It just isn't fair," Coretta thought. She remembered thinking the same thing years ago as she trudged along the dirt road to school. Black children in the area went to the Crossroads School in Heiberger. No matter how far away they lived, they had to walk. Every day, rain or shine, Coretta had to walk 3 miles to school and 3 miles home again. Every day, the school bus rumbled past, carrying white children to their school.

"Why can't I ride the bus, Mama?" Coretta had asked one day. Sadly, her mother had taken her in her arms and tried to explain. "You are just as good as anyone else. It's just the way things are."

"But it isn't fair," Coretta had protested.

She knew that the white children had a fine brick school with separate rooms for each grade. They even had a library. At the Crossroads School over a hundred children were crowded into one shabby room. Two teachers struggled to teach all 6 grades. There were never enough books to go around.

With these handicaps, it wasn't easy for the children at Coretta's school to finish all 6 grades. It was almost impossible for them to go to high school. The nearest black high school was 20 miles away. No buses were provided to reach it although white students were bussed 10 miles to Marion High School.

Coretta's mother had only a fourth grade education herself, but she was determined that her children would go to high school. She felt that if they got a good education, they might have a chance to escape some of the hardships black people faced in Alabama.

She arranged for Coretta and Edythe to stay with a family in Marion, so that they could go to a private high school there. At first the Scott girls were the only black

children from their community to go to high school. Most families couldn't afford to pay for their children's room and board. When Coretta was a junior, her father converted one of his trucks into a bus. Although it meant a 40-mile trip each day, Mrs. Scott drove all the children from their area to and from school. After that Coretta was able to live at home.

Lincoln School opened a whole new world to Coretta. It was as good as the white high schools in the area. All the students were black, but some of the teachers were white. They believed that black children deserved as good an education as white children. Other white people in Marion hated the white teachers. They threatened them and called them names for daring to live and work with black people.

Coretta saw that her teachers at Lincoln were willing to take great risks to help black people. She began to feel that what her mother had said was true — that she really was "as good as anybody else."

Coretta's new-found faith in herself was soon tested. To earn some extra money, she got a job in Marion, doing housework for a white woman. The woman expected Coretta to use the back door and to say, "Yes, ma'am," whenever she was spoken to. Coretta couldn't bring herself to do either. She lost the job.

At Lincoln, Coretta earned top grades in all her subjects, but music was her first love. In grade school her teachers had discovered that she had an unusually fine voice, and she had often been asked to sing solos for visitors. At Lincoln she took voice lessons and also sang in the choir. She learned to play the trumpet and the piano.

In her senior year at Lincoln, Coretta won a scholarship to Antioch College in Yellow Springs, Ohio. She was tremendously excited. Surely in a northern college she would be able to get away from the race problem. Surely there she would be treated the same as anyone else.

At first, Antioch was all Coretta had hoped for. The white students tried to be friendly and helpful. But Coretta found that even at a northern college there was a race barrier. Even at Antioch there were students who felt that black people were inferior. They were careful to assure Coretta, "Of course, Corrie, *you're* different." But she was hurt, just the same.

In college Coretta continued her studies in music. She decided to become a teacher. She was the first black student to major in education. Although there were black children in the Yellow Springs public schools, there were no black teachers. The school board refused to accept Coretta as a practice teacher. Her teaching supervisor was not willing to push the matter. When she appealed to the president of the college, she was told she would have to teach in the private school run by the college.

Coretta was angry and disillusioned. But she told herself, "Now I'm going to be black the rest of my life, and I have to face these problems. So I'm not going to let this one get me down."

She accepted the fact that she could not teach in a public school. But she vowed that she would work to change the situation. Antioch had a Race Relations Committee and several other student groups concerned with equal rights for black people. Coretta joined all of them. She was determined that black students who came after her would be treated fairly.

In her last year at Antioch, Coretta's teachers urged her to continue her studies in music. They thought she was talented enough to become a concert singer. Before graduation, she applied for a grant to study at the New England Conservatory of Music in Boston.

A letter soon arrived. Coretta had been accepted at the Conservatory. But weeks passed without word about the money. Fall came. Coretta still had heard nothing. Finally, with only 15 dollars in her purse, she boarded the train for Boston. She was determined to work at any job she could find to earn money to pay for her musical studies.

At the last minute, Coretta's grant did come through. But it covered only her fees at the Conservatory. After Coretta found a room and paid for her first week's rent, she had almost nothing left for food. For several days she existed on peanut butter, graham crackers, and fruit. Finally, she found a job doing housework. Later a job with a mail order house helped her meet expenses.

Coretta was sometimes lonely in Boston. Her studies

and part-time jobs kept her so busy she didn't have much chance to meet people. One day a friend told her about a young man from Atlanta named Martin Luther King, Jr. "He's a minister studying at Boston University," her friend said. "He's very anxious to meet you."

When her friend mentioned that the young man was a minister, Coretta lost interest. She was sure he would be like the ministers she had known as a child—self-righteous and narrow-minded. "No, thank you," she said firmly.

Coretta's friend insisted that Martin Luther King was a very different kind of minister. Finally Coretta said Martin could call her. He did; and as they talked, Coretta became

interested in spite of herself. She agreed to have lunch with him.

When Martin drove up in his green Chevrolet, Coretta's first thought was, "He's so short." However, she soon forgot his height. She began to feel that he was a very special person.

Martin was equally impressed with her. On the way home he told her, "You have everything I have ever wanted in a wife." Coretta was so surprised she could hardly reply. But when he asked if he could see her again, she said yes. Soon they were spending as much time together as their studies would allow. But whenever Martin mentioned marriage, Coretta changed the subject.

She wanted to be a concert singer, not a minister's wife. Yet the more Martin talked about his goals in life, the more

Coretta came to feel that they were the same as hers. He, too, wanted to help poor people get a good education and decent jobs. He, too, wanted to help black people gain their freedom. Finally Coretta decided to marry Martin even though it might mean she would not have the career she'd planned on.

Less than a year later Coretta and Martin were married in a simple ceremony at her family's home in Alabama. After the wedding the couple returned to Boston to complete their studies.

That winter Martin had offers of positions from 2 northern churches and 2 in the South. He and Coretta knew their life would be much easier in the North. After the freedom of Boston, it would be difficult to go back to the segregated South, where they would be treated like second-class citizens. But it was in the South where change was most needed. Coretta and Martin decided it was their duty to return. Martin accepted the pastorate of the Dexter Avenue Baptist Church in Montgomery, Alabama.

Segregation in Montgomery was even more degrading than Coretta had remembered. She and Martin had to use elevators, drinking fountains, and rest rooms marked "colored." They had to eat in "colored" restaurants. They couldn't even enter public buildings by the same door as white people.

Of all the unjust rules, none were worse than those of the Montgomery Bus Company. The first seats on all buses were for whites. Black people had to sit in the rear. If the front seats were filled and more white people boarded the bus, blacks had to get up and give them their seats. Black people had to pay their fares at the front of the bus, get off, and get on again by the rear door. Sometimes the bus would drive off without them after they had paid their fares.

Coretta and Martin talked the situation over. "What would happen if black people stopped riding the buses as a protest?" Martin wondered. He suggested his idea to friends. They thought it might work *some day*.

Then on December 1, 1955, Mrs. Rosa Parks refused to give up her seat on a bus to a white man. She was arrested and taken to jail. Suddenly black citizens of Montgomery decided they had had enough. Black leaders accepted Martin's idea of a bus boycott. The old mimeograph machine at his Dexter Avenue Church printed out a message to the city's 50,000 black people: "Don't ride the bus to work, to town, to school, or anywhere, Monday, December 5."

On December 5, Martin and Coretta King were up at 5:30 a.m. The first bus was due past their house at 6:00. As its headlights pierced the darkness, Coretta stood at the window, straining to see inside. "Martin, it's empty!" she exclaimed. There was not one person on the usually crowded bus. Hardly anyone rode the bus that day. Some people got to work by car, some by horse-drawn buggy. Thousands walked.

That afternoon black leaders met again. They drew up

a list of demands. They didn't ask that black people be able to sit anywhere they wanted on buses — only that bus drivers treat them politely and that black people not be forced to give up their seats to whites.

That night a mass meeting was held. Five thousand people came. They agreed to continue the boycott until the demands were met. Black citizens of Montgomery knew they were in for a long struggle.

The Kings' house became the headquarters of the protest movement. At all hours of the day or night groups of people were meeting there. It was a hectic time for Coretta. Although she had a new baby to care for, she made and accepted hundreds of phone calls to co-ordinate the plans for the boycott. The phone rang from 5:00 a.m. till past midnight. Often when Coretta answered, she heard someone threatening to kill her or her husband. As the protest movement grew, the frightening calls increased.

One evening in January, Martin left to speak at a meeting. Because of the telephone threats, a friend came to stay with Coretta. About 9:30 p.m., as the 2 women sat chatting in the living room, there was a thump on the front porch. Frightened, Coretta and her friend ran toward the back bedroom where the baby was sleeping. As they ran, there was a tremendous explosion and the sound of breaking glass.

Then the doorbell rang. For a terrible moment, Coretta feared the person who had thrown the bomb was at the

door. Then a friendly voice called, "Anybody hurt?" Neighbors came running into the smoke-filled house, relieved to find Coretta and the baby safe.

The sound of the explosion had been heard many blocks away. By the time Martin arrived home, an angry crowd had gathered on the Kings' front lawn. Armed with guns, knives, and broken bottles, they were determined to seek revenge. In a calm voice Martin told them to put down their weapons. He persuaded them to return peacefully to their homes. But both he and Coretta were badly shaken by the experience.

The bombing was the most severe test yet of Coretta's commitment to the protest movement. Her family and Martin's tried to persuade her to take the baby and leave Montgomery for a time. She refused. As the days went by, she felt more and more strongly that the struggle for freedom was a cause worth any risk—even death.

The bus boycott lasted over a year. Finally, a Supreme Court order ended segregation on Montgomery buses. By that time requests were pouring in from all across the nation for Martin Luther King to help organize other non-violent protests. The boycott had shown what black people could do if they forgot their fears and stood together. Many white people also joined the "peaceful war" for equality. The civil rights movement spread from Montgomery to Atlanta and Birmingham, and finally north to Chicago and New York.

Reluctantly Martin Luther King resigned his position

at the Dexter Avenue Church in Montgomery. The Kings moved to Atlanta so that Martin could head a new organization called the Southern Christian Leadership Conference (SCLC), which was based there. The family moved into a modest brick house in one of Atlanta's poorer neighborhoods.

Martin had been offered many jobs with high salaries, but he had turned them down. He took no money from the SCLC and accepted only enough money for the family to live on from his father's Ebenezer Baptist Church, where he was co-pastor. Coretta didn't mind not having a large house or expensive furniture. She and Martin both believed that it was what a person did to help people that was important, not what he was able to buy.

As her family and the civil rights movement grew, so did demands on Coretta King. After Yolanda, Martin Luther King, III (Marty) was born. Then came Dexter and Bernice (Bunny). With 4 small children to care for, Coretta was busy at home. Yet she was often asked to travel with Martin and to give concerts and speeches herself. Somehow she found the strength to do all these things.

Coretta found a way to use her musical talent in the struggle for equal rights. She gave a concert at New York's Town Hall, using poetry, dramatic readings, protest songs, and old Negro spirituals to tell the story of the civil rights movement. The combination of words and song was effective and inspiring. Soon Coretta began getting requests from all

over the country for more "Freedom Concerts." She found herself singing to audiences of as many as 10,000 people.

Besides helping people understand the civil rights movement, Coretta's concerts provided a much-needed source of funds. At one point there was so little money in the SCLC treasury, Martin was afraid they wouldn't be able to pay his office staff that month. At the last moment a check for $2,000 from one of Coretta's concerts came in the mail. Another $6,000 was raised for the families of 3 young civil rights workers murdered in Mississippi. In all, Coretta raised more than $50,000, all of which she donated to the movement.

Coretta shared her husband's belief that problems could be solved without violence. She believed that the civil rights movement had to be seen as a small part in the larger cause of world peace. In 1962 she was asked to be a delegate to a peace conference in Geneva, Switzerland. There she

joined women from all over the world, meeting to urge the Russian and American governments to stop testing nuclear weapons.

Even though Coretta was busy traveling and giving concerts and speeches, the needs of her family always came first. More and more Martin's work took him away from home. Coretta fully understood the danger he faced daily. Each time they said goodby, she knew she might not see him again.

Over the years Coretta's courage was tested time and again. Once she got a phone call telling her Martin had been rushed to the hospital in New York. A mentally disturbed woman had stabbed him in the chest with a letter opener. Three hours of surgery were needed to remove the weapon. Afterwards doctors told Coretta that its point had been touching Martin's heart. If he had panicked and moved suddenly or even sneezed, he would have died instantly. Even after the successful surgery, he remained on the critical list for several days.

Though terribly worried, Coretta remained calm. When Martin began to recover, she took his place at meetings and gave speeches from his notes. Many people credit her with holding the movement together during this critical time.

Shortly before Dexter was born, Coretta again feared for her husband's life. He was arrested for leading a sit-in at a lunch counter in Atlanta. For this minor offense, the judge handed down a harsh sentence of 6 months hard labor at the State Penitentiary.

Coretta was terribly upset. The penitentiary was 300 miles from the Kings' home in Atlanta. Pregnant and with 2 small children, she could rarely make the 8-hour trip to visit her husband. She knew how black prisoners were treated in southern jails. Martin might be beaten — or worse.

Before lawyers had time to appeal the judge's decision, Martin was roughly dragged from his Atlanta jail cell. He was chained and handcuffed. In the middle of the night, he was taken to the penitentiary.

When Coretta heard what had happened, she was distraught. Just as she was about to give up hope, the telephone rang. "Just a moment, Mrs. King," the long-distance operator said. "Senator John F. Kennedy wants to speak to you."

"How are you, Mrs. King?" a warm voice inquired. After chatting a few minutes about her family and the new baby they were expecting, Senator Kennedy told Coretta he was concerned about Martin's arrest. "Let me know if there's anything I can do to help," he told her. The next day, Martin was released.

Two years later, Coretta had another talk with John Kennedy. By then he was President. Martin had been jailed in Birmingham. Coretta was not allowed to see or even phone him. Fearing the worst, she called the White House. Once again Kennedy came to the rescue, and Martin was freed.

Through all the dark moments of her life, Coretta never doubted that the cause to which she and Martin had dedicat-

ed their lives was right. Even on April 4, 1968, when she faced the supreme test — the death of her husband — her faith never wavered. She had suffered much. A lesser woman might have withdrawn from the world in grief. Coretta did .not.

The day after Martin was shot, Coretta made an eloquent statement to the press. She said that both she and Martin had accepted the fact that his life might suddenly be cut short. They both felt it wasn't how long one lived that was important, but how well. Martin Luther King had given his life, trying to help people find a better way to solve their problems than by hatred and violence. Coretta urged those who had loved and admired her husband to help carry on the work he had begun.

The day before his funeral, Coretta took Martin's place in the march he was to lead in Memphis. From all over the country thousands of people came to march with her. Thousands more stood along the route in silent tribute to the memory of their leader and the bravery of his widow.

Coretta's faith carried her heroically through the ordeal of Martin's funeral. Throughout the long hours of speeches and television coverage, she never broke down. All who saw her marveled at her serenity and inner strength.

In the months after her husband's death, Coretta fulfilled the commitments he didn't live to meet. At a peace rally in New York, she spoke from his notes. She launched his Poor People's Campaign from Memphis. Later, from the steps of the Lincoln Memorial in Washington, D.C., she reminded a crowd of 50,000 poor people of the dream of peace and freedom Martin Luther King had described there 5 years earlier.

Coretta got more invitations than she could accept. She traveled to India, Jamaica, and Italy to accept awards in her husband's behalf. In Rome, she had an audience with Pope Paul VI. In London, she became the first woman ever invited to speak at St. Paul's Cathedral. At a Washington National Symphony Concert, Coretta narrated Aaron Copland's "A Lincoln Portrait."

Today Coretta does not dwell on the past. She is too much involved in the present. But she is never too busy for her 4 children. They are the most important people in her life. She limits all her other activities so that she can spend most of her time with them. It is to Coretta's credit that despite the tragedy they have lived through, her children are happy and normal. In fact, one of Yolanda's school friends couldn't believe she was really Martin Luther King's daughter. She told Yolanda, "I thought you'd be all 'stuck up.' You're just like everybody else."

After her children, Coretta feels her most important concern is seeing that her husband's work is carried on. Almost immediately after his death, she began to plan a memorial for him. She had in mind, not a monument of stone, but a place filled with activity and life. She wanted to build a memorial center which would keep Martin Luther

King's memory and his teachings alive.

Little by little, Coretta is seeing her dream become a reality. The Martin Luther King, Jr. Center for Social Change has already been opened. It is located in the Atlanta neighborhood where he was born, where he carried out his work, and where he now is buried.

Workers at the center are helping black people register to vote. They are helping poor farm workers press for higher wages and better working conditions. They are trying to improve prisons. Scholars are recording the history of the civil rights movement. Children are learning about the history of black people in America.

Coretta King is president of the Center. She has done much of the planning and has worked hard to interest people in the project and to raise money for it.

Even when the center is finished, Coretta's work will go on. For her goal is no less than peace and freedom for all the world's peoples. She hopes to encourage more women to become leaders in government and social action. She feels that women should use their great capacity for love and self-sacrifice to help make this a better world.

Certainly this is what Coretta herself has done. As wife and mother, as musician and peace activist, she has accomplished a great deal. The wrongs she has suffered have not made her bitter, but compassionate. The tragedy she has lived through has made her strong. She is an inspiration to everyone.

Walt Disney
Bob Hope
Duke Ellington
Dwight Eisenhower
Coretta King
Pablo Picasso
Ralph Nader
Bill Cosby
Dag Hammarskjold
Sir Frederick Banting
Mark Twain
Beatrix Potter

# close
# ups